W9-BAY-759

Plants
AND
Animals

AUTHORS

Mary Atwater
The University of Georgia

Prentice Baptiste
University of Georgia

Lucy Daniel
Rutherford County Schools

Jay Hackett
University of Northern Colorado

Richard Moyer
University of Michigan, Dearborn

Carol Takemoto
Los Angeles Unified School District

Nancy Wilson
Sacramento Unified School District

Lion

Macmillan/McGraw-Hill School Publishing Company

New York   Columbus

MACMILLAN / McGRAW-HILL

SCIENCE TURNS MINDS ON ™

CONSULTANTS

Assessment:

Janice M. Camplin
Curriculum Coordinator, Elementary Science
Mentor, Western New York
Lake Shore Central Schools
Angola, NY

Mary Hamm
Associate Professor
Department of Elementary Education
San Francisco State University
San Francisco, CA

Cognitive Development:

Dr. Elisabeth Charron
Assistant Professor of Science Education
Montana State University
Bozeman, MT

Sue Teele
Director of Education Extension
University of California, Riverside
Riverside, CA

Cooperative Learning:

Harold Pratt
Executive Director of Curriculum
Jefferson County Public Schools
Golden, CO

Earth Science:

Thomas A. Davies
Research Scientist
The University of Texas
Austin, TX

David G. Futch
Associate Professor of Biology
San Diego State University
San Diego, CA

Dr. Shadia Rifai Habbal
Harvard-Smithsonian Center for Astrophysics
Cambridge, MA

Tom Murphree, Ph.D.
Global Systems Studies
Monterey, CA

Suzanne O'Connell
Assistant Professor
Wesleyan University
Middletown, CT

Environmental Education:

Cheryl Charles, Ph.D.
Executive Director
Project Wild
Boulder, CO

Gifted:

Sandra N. Kaplan
Associate Director, National/State Leadership
Training Institute on the Gifted/Talented
Ventura County Superintendent of Schools Office
Northridge, CA

Global Education:

M. Eugene Gilliom
Professor of Social Studies and Global Education
The Ohio State University
Columbus, OH

Merry M. Merryfield
Assistant Professor of Social Studies and Global
Education
The Ohio State University
Columbus, OH

Intermediate Specialist

Sharon L. Strating
Missouri State Teacher of the Year
Northwest Missouri State University
Marysville, MO

Life Science:

Carl D. Barrentine
Associate Professor of Biology
California State University
Bakersfield, CA

V.L. Holland
Professor and Chair, Biological Sciences
Department
California Polytechnic State University
San Luis Obispo, CA

Donald C. Lisowy
Education Specialist
New York, NY

Dan B. Walker
Associate Dean for Science Education and
Professor of Biology
San Jose State University
San Jose, CA

Literature:

Dr. Donna E. Norton
Texas A&M University
College Station, TX

Tina Thoburn, Ed.D.
President
Thoburn Educational Enterprises, Inc.
Ligonier, PA

Macmillan/McGraw-Hill School Division
10 Union Square East
New York, New York 10003

Printed in the United States of America

ISBN 0-02-276117-9/4

5 6 7 8 9 VHJ 99 98 97 96

Mathematics:

Martin L. Johnson
Professor, Mathematics Education
University of Maryland at College Park
College Park, MD

Physical Science:

Max Diem, Ph.D.
Professor of Chemistry
City University of New York, Hunter College
New York, NY

Gretchen M. Gillis
Geologist
Maxus Exploration Company
Dallas, TX

Wendell H. Potter
Associate Professor of Physics
Department of Physics
University of California, Davis
Davis, CA

Claudia K. Viehland
Educational Consultant, Chemist
Sigma Chemical Company
St. Louis, MO

Reading:

Jean Wallace Gillet
Reading Teacher
Charlottesville Public Schools
Charlottesville, VA

Charles Temple, Ph. D.
Associate Professor of Education
Hobart and William Smith Colleges
Geneva, NY

Safety:

Janice Sutkus
Program Manager: Education

National Safety Council
Chicago, IL

Science Technology and Society (STS):

William C. Kyle, Jr.
Director, School Mathematics and Science Center
Purdue University
West Lafayette, IN

Social Studies:

Mary A. McFarland
Instructional Coordinator of
Social Studies, K-12, and
Director of Staff Development
Parkway School District
St. Louis, MO

Lily

Students Acquiring English:

Mrs. Bronwyn G. Frederick, M.A.
Bilingual Teacher
Pomona Unified School District
Pomona, CA

Misconceptions:

Dr. Charles W. Anderson
Michigan State University
East Lansing, MI

Dr. Edward L. Smith
Michigan State University
East Lansing, MI

Multicultural:

Bernard L. Charles
Senior Vice President
Quality Education for Minorities Network
Washington, DC

Cheryl Willis Hudson
Graphic Designer and Publishing Consultant
Part Owner and Publisher, Just Us Books, Inc.
Orange, NJ

Paul B. Janeczko
Poet
Hebron, MA

James R. Murphy
Math Teacher
La Guardia High School
New York, NY

Ramon L. Santiago
Professor of Education and Director of ESL
Lehman College, City University of New York
Bronx, NY

Clifford E. Trafzer
Professor and Chair, Ethnic Studies
University of California, Riverside
Riverside, CA

STUDENT ACTIVITY TESTERS

Jennifer Kildow
Brooke Straub
Cassie Zistl
Betsy McKeown
Seth McLaughlin
Max Berry
Wayne Henderson

FIELD TEST TEACHERS

Sharon Ervin
San Pablo Elementary School
Jacksonville, FL

Michelle Gallaway
Indianapolis Public School #44
Indianapolis, IN

Kathryn Gallman
#7 School
Rochester, NY

Karla McBride
#44 School
Rochester, NY

Diane Pease
Leopold Elementary
Madison, WI

Kathy Perez
Martin Luther King Elementary
Jacksonville, FL

Ralph Stamler
Thoreau School
Madison, WI

Joanne Stern
Hilltop Elementary School
Glen Burnie, MD

Janet Young
Indianapolis Public School #90
Indianapolis, IN

CONTRIBUTING WRITER

Don Schaub

Plants and Animals

Activities!

EXPLORE

TRY THIS

Features

Links

Music/Art Link

Literature Links

Social Studies Links

Focus on Technology

Focus on Environment

Departments

Plants and Animals

Foraminifera, a tiny protozoan

African elephants

Elephants are the largest land animals on Earth today. They grow from 3 to 3.5 meters tall (about 10 to 11 feet) and weigh up to 6 metric tons (about 7 tons). Blue whales are even bigger. They may grow 30 meters long (about 100 feet) and weigh 135 metric tons (about 150 tons). The heaviest flower we know about is the rafflesia, which grows in the tropical forests of southeast Asia. It weighs as much as 9 kilograms (about 20 pounds), measures from 0.9 to 1.2 meters in diameter (about 3 to 4 feet), and it smells bad!

You can't see the smallest living things without a microscope. They have only one cell. Scientists have probably not yet discovered many of the living things that share Earth with us. Living things come in many shapes and sizes, but they have some basic things in common.

All living things are made of cells. By the time you are fully grown, your body will contain about 100 trillion (100,000,000,000,000) cells! Think how many cells an elephant must have. But one-celled organisms are made of cells, too.

The first traces of life on Earth date back over 3 billion years. Every living thing since that time has carried on certain life functions such as growth and reproduction. Over a long period of time, life evolved from its earliest signs to its present forms.

It is the diversity of the life-forms that have evolved over time that you will be exploring in this unit. To understand similarities and differences, and to explain how living things have changed over time, scientists have organized and classified living things into different groups. This requires careful observation of the similarities and differences among living things.

Activity!

Life Around You

What You Need
Activity Log page 1

Look around you. In your *Activity Log*, list at least ten living things you see or you can think of. Like a scientist, think carefully about the similarities and differences among these living things. In your *Activity Log,* organize or classify your living things based on your observations. Now name the groups of living things you classified. Discuss your list with your classmates.

In the Try This Activity, you made up your own system of classification. How did you go about placing living things in groups? Did you have plants and animals? Did you have any other groups? Did you look at how they are made? Do they all have the same parts?

A system of classifying living things that people have been using for many years identifies five different groups or kingdoms. More groups may be added as people become aware of further differences among living things. In this unit you are going to explore only two of the kingdoms: plants and animals.

Minds On! In your *Activity Log* on page 2, write down as many reasons as you can for classifying plants and animals. Look back at your list from the Try This Activity. Did you classify living things in that activity for the same reasons that you did in this one? Why or why not? Did you classify plants and animals that are used as food? We don't just need plants and animals for food. How else do you interact with them? What would your life be like without them? ●

Why would you want to understand more about plants and animals?

Metro Park
Saturday, 2:30 pm

Gray Squirrel

Praying Mantis

Moss

Pine

Mountains. Deserts. Forests. Beaches. Valleys. Plains. Swamplands. Rain forests. Think of all the places to live on Earth. Even if you live in a city, it's probably in one of these environments. Where do you live? Think about the types of plants that share your part of Earth with you. What parts do they have that make them suited to survive in the same place you do?

What's the Point of Plant Parts?

What's the strangest place you've ever seen a plant growing? It sometimes seems as though plants can grow everywhere. You find them in your house, in your yard, and even in the cracks of highways. Some grow in swamps or oceans. Some grow in the dry desert. Some plants thrive under the snow and others live in forests or swamps.

Think about some of the plants you have eaten recently. Do you know how each plant uses its parts to survive? If plants have the same kinds of parts, why do you think the parts of one plant look different from the same parts of another plant?

Scientists do not just guess at or make up explanations for things. They observe something carefully and then use the information to make an educated guess or **hypothesis** (hī poth´ ə sis). Scientists may then choose to test the hypothesis in an experiment. You can hypothesize about plant parts in the next activity.

TRY THIS

Activity!

Why Are Plant Parts Different?

Try observing like a scientist to hypothesize about the different uses of plant parts.

What You Need

three different plants: a succulent, a water, and a flowering plant, such as a cactus, a duckweed, and a geranium; *Activity Log* page 3

Look at the physical properties of the leaves of each plant. What color are they? What size and shape are they? How do they feel? How do they smell? List any other plant parts you see. Observe the physical properties of these parts. Record your observations in your *Activity Log*.

Now use your observations to try to answer these questions. How do the parts of the cactus help it survive in a hot, dry desert? Would the geranium be able to survive in the desert? Could the duckweed survive out of water? Could these plants survive outside where you live? Why or why not?

Plant Needs

Plants have different types of roots. Roots can be thick like carrots or have many branches like the roots of trees and grasses. But roots perform the same function for all plants and work with other plant parts to maintain the plant. Some plant parts work to help the plant grow. Others help the plant **reproduce** (rē´ prə düs´), or make new plants. Keep this in mind as you examine why the same parts vary in size and shape in different plants.

Minds On! Touch your nose. Do you feel your breath going in and out? Do you feel your skin? Think about how many parts of your body are working together to perform this simple action. What kinds of parts does a plant have to meet its needs? What are some things you think a plant needs to live and grow? Write your answers on page 6 in your *Activity Log.* ●

Plants also get nutrients from other living things. When plants and animals die, they decay and release their nutrients, which return to the soil.

When you look at a plant, you may not see much happening. But, like people and animals, plants have needs. Living things exist on Earth because Earth has certain conditions that allow them to grow and reproduce: light, air, water, and space.

Plants also need **nutrients** (nü´ trē ənts), or certain substances found in soil, to live. Some nutrients come from rocks, which are filled with minerals. Minerals are not living but they contain compounds that plants use as nutrients. These nutrients become part of the soil when rock minerals break up into very small pieces and dissolve.

People and animals learn to stay away from plants that have poison or thorns. The stems, leaves, and roots of poison ivy contain oils that can irritate skin and cause swelling.

Adaptations

Plants that live in different environments have different characteristics that allow them to survive. Over time, adaptations or changes in plant parts have occurred, and they continue to occur to increase the chances that plant species can survive in their environments. Anything that helps an organism survive in its environment is an **adaptation** (ad´ əp tā´ shən). Adaptations are what make the sizes and shapes of plant parts different.

Because they stay in one place, plants must be able to get what they need from their surroundings. Think of all the different types of environments where plants live.

Some plants have adaptations that help them survive.

Plants in the far north grow close to the ground as protection from the wind.

Desert plants grow far apart so that they can get water and nutrients from a larger area. The sharp spines of a cactus keep animals from eating it.

Invent a Plant   Music/Art Link

Try inventing your own kind of plant for the environment in which you live. This will give you a clearer picture of how a plant adapts to its environment. With three other students, discuss what kinds of parts and adaptations you want to give your plant so that it will survive in your environment. Draw a picture of your plant. Discuss the function of each part of your plant. Draw the plant in your *Activity Log* on page 7 and label the parts that help it adapt to your environment.

Activity!

Observing "Breathing" Plants

Tiny openings in the leaves allow plants to take in carbon dioxide and to give off oxygen and water.

What You Need

leaf, hand lens, jar, water, *Activity Log* page 8

Fill the jar with water and submerge the leaf in the water. Observe the leaf for five minutes. Observe the leaf with a hand lens. Record your observations in your *Activity Log.*

What appears on the leaf? Do you think it came from the water or the leaf? How is what you saw important in photosynthesis and respiration?

Plant Parts

Each part of a plant has certain functions. Leaves, stems, and roots work together as a system to help the plant perform its life functions.

Leaves

Plants don't eat food as you do. They make their own food and provide food for other living things. Most of the food is made inside the leaves.

Roots

The structures that hold the plant in the ground are called **roots** *(rüts). Roots also provide the plant with water and with nutrients that have dissolved in the water. Roots absorb water and nutrients from the soil, and without these the plant could not survive. What types of roots have you seen in your environment?*

Food to Energy

Chlorophyll is used in **photosynthesis** (fō´ tə sin´ thə sis), the process by which green plants make food. In photosynthesis, light energy and certain chemicals are used to change water and carbon dioxide into sugar and oxygen. The roots absorb water and the leaves absorb carbon dioxide. The chlorophyll inside the leaf absorbs light energy. The oxygen is given off into the air through openings in the leaf and the sugar is used as food.

Respiration (res´ pə rā´ shən) is the process by which a plant uses oxygen to change food into the energy it needs for life functions.

*Nearly all plant leaves are green because they contain a chemical called **chlorophyll** (klôr´ ə fil´).*

Stems

*Getting water and nutrients from the roots to the rest of the plant is the job of the **stems** (stemz). Stems also hold plants up so that the leaves can get sunlight. Some stems store nutrients and water for the plant.*

Other Plant Uses

Plant part adaptations matter to you in ways you have probably never thought of. Many of the medicines you take when you are sick come from plant parts. Look around you. Do you see any wooden furniture? It is made from the stems of trees. The paper you are looking at right now comes from the same source.

Because of plant adaptations, we also have a variety of foods to eat. Think of all the different foods you like. How many are plants or plant products? Could animals survive without plant foods?

Plants Around the World   Social Studies Link

Look at the pictures on this page. Decide if the plant is adapted to a cold or a hot environment. Locate places on a globe that each plant might come from. Discuss your conclusions with your classmates.

What are your favorite types of stems, leaves, and roots? You eat more of these than you think.

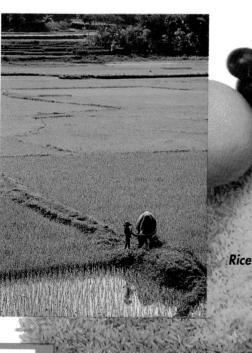

Rice paddy

Rice

Banana

◀ *Banana tree*

Spinach plant

◀ Spinach

◀ Cranberries

Cranberry plant

Sum It Up

Earth has a variety of environments. A particular type of plant cannot live in every environment on Earth. When you move a plant, such as a cactus, away from its natural environment, you may have to make special arrangements for it. It can't survive in a cold, wet place. Plants that grow where you live would have trouble living in very different environments, too. Their leaves, stems, and roots have adapted to their environment over a long period of time, and any big change could destroy them.

Critical Thinking

1. What plants grow well where you live? How are they adapted to your environment?
2. How can plant adaptations improve the quality of life for people?
3. What could happen to plants if an Earth environment changed from cold to hot?

Flowers for
All Occasions

Like stems, leaves, and roots, the flowers of plants come in all shapes, sizes, and colors. The colors, sizes, and shapes are not just for show. They are important to the survival of the plant.

Minds On! In your *Activity Log* on page 9, draw a picture of your favorite flower. Then, if you can, write its name and label its parts. ●

Plenty of Plants

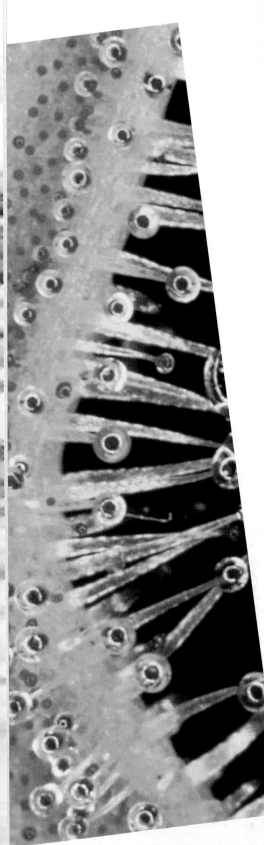

What if you found a plant no one had ever seen before? It could happen. No one really knows how many plants there are on Earth. How would you tell other people about your discovery? How could you compare it to some other plant or animal they already know?

Big plants. Small plants. We eat some of them and build houses with others. Some have flowers. Some are poisonous. There are more than 260,000 different kinds of plants. People are still finding new ones.

People want to make sense out of the world. Even little babies sort or classify food plants they like from ones they don't like. Can you think of other ways people classify things?

What would you say about your plant discovery? You might talk about some of its physical properties—taste, color, size, and shape. What else would you use to classify it?

Minds On! Think about the system you use to organize your things at home and at school. Do you have a collection of baseball cards, rocks, coins, dolls, or stamps? How do you organize your clothes? On page 15 in your *Activity Log,* make a list or draw pictures of the ways you classify your things. Could you use any of these ways to classify your newly discovered plant? Think about how a plant uses its parts to live. That might give you another clue about how to classify it. ●

The sundew plant is able to trap bugs and digest them. However, the mirid bug is able to live on this plant and help eat the trapped bugs without becoming trapped itself.

Why Are Animals

Animals, like plants, come in many shapes and sizes. And, like plants, animals have certain basic needs that must be met if they are to survive. This lesson examines how animals are adapted to get the things they need from their environment.

Finding a flea on this lion is no easy matter. A flea is so small you can barely see it. You wouldn't have any trouble seeing the giant blue whale. It's as big as five elephants and weighs up to 135 metric tons (about 150 tons). The flea and the whale don't exactly look like cousins, but both are animals. Both need food, water, and air to survive. No matter how large or how small, every animal has what it takes to find food, to protect itself from its enemies, and to survive in its environment.

Built That Way?

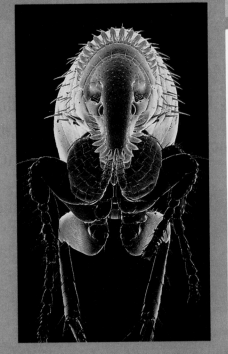

Minds On! If an elephant wants the leaves off a tree, it uses its strong trunk to pull the tree down. How would a monkey get those leaves? How would an insect? What about a giraffe? Write your answers on page 20 in your *Activity Log.* ●

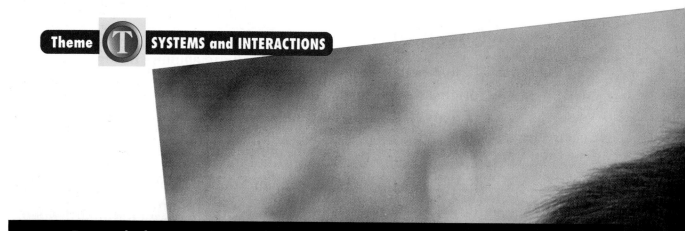

Bear cubs learn to climb trees to get away from their enemies, and some chimpanzees use twigs to get termites out of rotten logs so that they have food to eat. How do they know how to do these things?

Have you ever seen a dog do tricks? If so, you know that animals can learn to do things. In Thailand and Malaysia, monkeys are taught to climb trees and pick coconuts on coconut plantations. The monkeys can pick as many as 500 coconuts a day. Botanist E. J. H. Corner used the same kind of monkey to climb trees and break off small branches so that he could study the flowers and leaves. You know that animals have certain parts that help them get food, move from place to place, and escape enemies. Animals also have certain behaviors that help them survive in their environments.

What Makes
Animals Behave
The Way They Do?

Instinct

Instincts are behaviors animals are born with. For example, bees are born knowing how to make honey. A spider knows right away how to spin a web to catch its food. A kitten turns to its mother for milk. A bird knows how to make a nest. Animals know how to find food, mate to produce offspring, and raise their young.

Animals migrate, or move to better conditions, by instinct. Some frogs migrate a few kilometers, while the Arctic tern migrates as much as 35,000 kilometers. Other animals, such as seals, whales, salmon, and deer, migrate in search of food and a safe place to live and raise their young. How do they know where to go? Instinct.

Geese fly together as they move from one area to another in search of food and a warmer climate.

Another instinct that animals have to survive cold weather and lack of food is hibernation. **Hibernation** (hī´ bər nā´ shən) is a deep sleep that helps bats, woodchucks, snakes, and other animals live through the winter. During hibernation the animals need very little energy to survive and can live off the fat they've stored in their bodies. Squirrels and raccoons do not hibernate but they do go into a deep sleep. Instead of sleeping all winter, they wake up to feed. Do the Try This Activity to see how other kinds of animals react when it's dark.

Hibernating bat

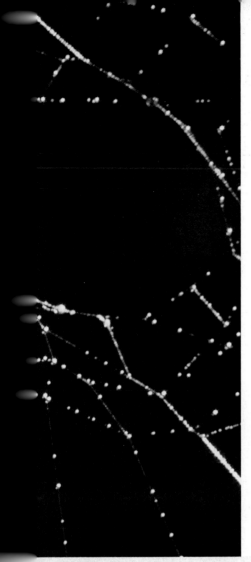

Silk Stronger Than Steel

Did you ever walk into a spider web? You probably think that those thin strands of spider silk are pretty weak. Scientists have learned that, ounce for ounce, spider silk is stronger than steel. That's not surprising when you remember that the spider depends on its web for food. The web has to catch large bugs flying into it at a high rate of speed. The web not only has to be strong, it has to stretch. A spider web can stretch to about ten times its original size. The spider's ability to produce such a strong food trap quickly and without special materials is its own food-getting adaptation.

TRY THIS Activity! In the Dark

Do earthworms like light or dark places?

What You Need
paper, index card, 3 or 4 earthworms, *Activity Log* page 28

You will observe the behavior of earthworms when they are placed in a new environment. Place a sheet of paper on a table. Fold the index card to look like a tent and place it on one end of the paper. Put an earthworm on the other end of the paper. Observe the movement of the earthworm for three minutes, then record your observations in your *Activity Log.* Repeat the experiment with two or three other earthworms. How do the earthworms react to their new environment? Can you explain how this is an example of instinct?

Learned Behaviors

You have seen examples of instincts, or behaviors that animals are born knowing. If you have ever tried to train a dog to do tricks, you know that not all behaviors are instincts. **Learned behavior** is behavior that is changed by experience.

A rat can learn to follow a certain path in a maze, a bird called a macaw can learn to talk, and you can learn to do lots of things.

Minds On! How many things have you learned to do? Talk with another student about all the things you have learned to do. These are examples of learned behaviors. How have they helped you? Write your answers on page 29 in your *Activty Log.* ●

Teaching animals certain behaviors can be very helpful. One example of how learned behavior can help us is the training of capuchin monkeys. Capuchins live in the tropical forests of Central and South America. Capuchins are now being trained to help disabled people. They go through a six-month training program where they learn 50 to 100 tasks. The trained capuchins are then given to disabled people to help with tasks such as opening and closing doors and windows, and fetching objects.

Sum It Up

Behaviors are very important for the survival of animals. Some animals live in groups to help them find food, stay warm, and remain safe from enemies. They have a much better chance of surviving in a group than they do if they are alone. Instincts also help animals in their surroundings. A bird knows how to build a nest, what materials to use, and where to build it. A strongly built nest on a high limb will protect the bird and its eggs from enemies.

You also learned the importance of another type of behavior—learned behavior. You have learned to do many things since you were born. These learned behaviors as well as your instincts help you live in your environment.

Critical Thinking

1. Can you think of things you do out of instinct? Can you think of behaviors you have learned?

2. What is similar about working with a group of classmates and living in a family?

3. How is the behavior of animals in a zoo similar to and different from the behavior of animals in the wild?

4. How are both zoo animals and wild animals different from pets?

Capuchin monkeys can be trained to aid people who are disabled.

63

Reach around and feel the middle of your back. What you feel is your backbone. What animals can you think of that have backbones? Would you be surprised to learn that most animals do not have backbones?

Theme Ⓣ **SCALE and STRUCTURE**

Can you imagine a zoo large enough to hold more than one million animals? That's how many kinds of animals there are in the world. There are lots of ways you could put animals into groups. Big ones. Small ones. Tame animals. Wild animals. Animals that live in the water. Animals that fly. In this lesson you will explore scientific ways of classifying animals.

Plants can be classified as vascular or nonvascular. Animals are also grouped according to the parts they have. But it's not an easy job. Libbie Henrietta Hyman (hī´ mən), a scientist working at the American Museum of Natural History, thought she could compile a record of all the animals without backbones in two big books. After more than 30 years of work and 6 volumes on different kinds of animals without backbones, her work was still unfinished. With so many animals around, can you see how difficult it would be to group all the animals in the world? There are also animals that have just been found and there are probably lots of animals that have not even been discovered yet.

Compass jellyfish

Minds On! Work with a partner to see how many animals you can list in five minutes. On your own, find a way to group the animals on your list. Compare your groups with your partner's. Did you find different ways of arranging the animals? Write your answers on page 30 in your *Activity Log.* ●

64

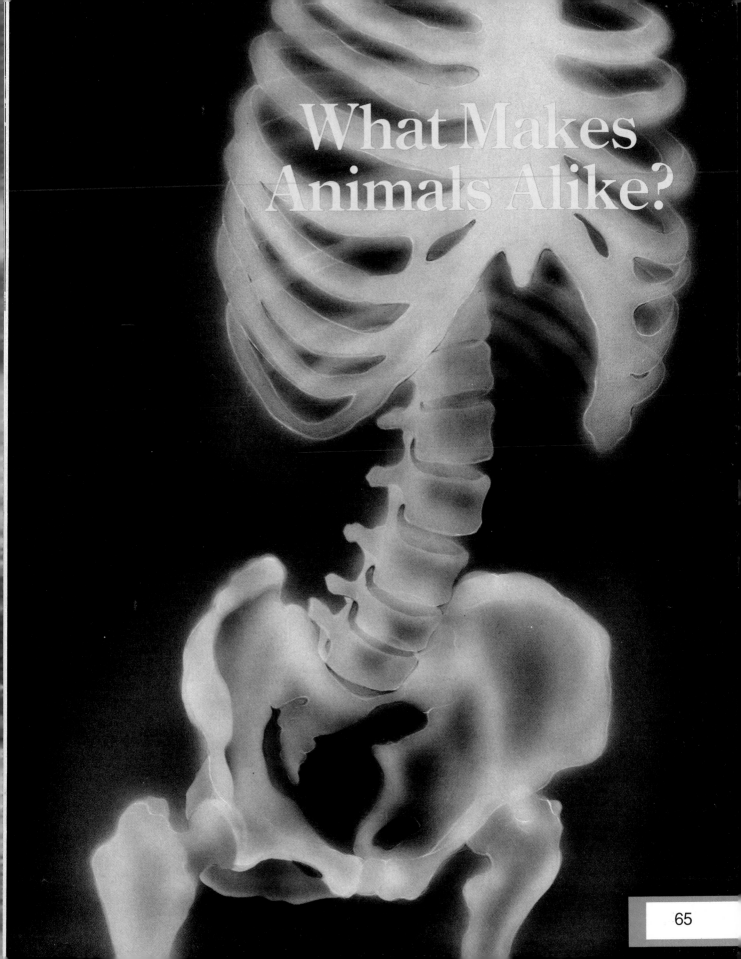

What Makes Animals Alike?

Animal Life Cycles

Animals grow up in very different ways. The life cycle in your activity with the fruit flies was different from that of a plant. It was different from your own life cycle or that of a dog or cat, too. Some animals, such as fruit flies, hatch from eggs. Other animals, like you and the dog or cat, are born alive. Below are the stages animals such as gorillas, humans, and whales go through.

Female rhinoceros and calf

Growth and Development

Childhood and adolescence in humans are the periods of growth and development. As animals get bigger, they learn to survive.

Beginning

Bears, lions, and humans are all born looking like small adults. Even young birds, fish, and reptiles such as snakes, turtles, and alligators hatch out of their eggs looking pretty much like their parents except for their color and size.

Death

Some animals die after reproducing. Others live many years after they lose the ability to reproduce. Both humans and elephants, on the average, live after they lose the ability to reproduce.

Reproduction

Adulthood is a time of reproduction and then aging. Most animals need both a male and a female to reproduce. But, like some plants, some animals, such as flatworms, can reproduce by breaking into two pieces. Each piece will grow into a whole flatworm again.

INDEX

CREDITS

Photo Credits:
Cover, The Image Bank/Lynn M. Stone; **1,** ©Frans Lanting/ALLSTOCK; **2, 3,** Animals Animals/Joe McDonald; **3,** ©Studiohio; **6,** (inset) ©Manfred Kage/Peter Arnold,Inc.; **6,7,** Bruce Coleman, Inc./Jen & Des Bartlett; **8, 9,** ©KS Studios; **9,** (itl) ©Larry Lefever/Grant Heilman Photography, Inc., (itr) ©Matt Meadows, (ibl) ©Jane Grushow/Grant Heilman Photography, Inc., (ibr) ©Grant Heilman Photography, Inc.; **10, 11,** ©Studiohio; **12, 13,** Wendy Shattil/Bob Rozinski ©1991; **14, 15,** ©Studiohio; **16, 17,** ©Milton Rand/Tom Stack & Associates; **17,** (it) ©John Cancalosi/Tom Stack & Associates, (im) ©George Herben/Alaskan Stock Images, (ib) Earth Scenes/John Lemker; **20,** (ibl) ©Gary Milburn/Tom Stack & Associates, (ibr) Earth Scenes/Zig Leszczynski; **20, 21,** ©Studiohio; **21,** (itl) Earth Scenes/E.R. Degginger, (ibl) Earth Scenes/Richard Kolar; **22, 23,** ©Studiohio; **24, 25, 26, 27,** ©Studiohio; **27,** (tr) ©Hans Pfletchinger/Peter Arnold, Inc.; **28,** (t) ©Studiohio, (ib) ©D. Smilea/Peter Arnold, Inc.; **29,** (tl) ©Studiohio, (mr) ©Matt Meadows/Peter Arnold, Inc., (bl) Earth Scenes/S. Dasher; **30,** (i) ©Kevin Schafer/Peter Arnold, Inc.; **30, 31,** ©Ken Lucas/Planet Earth Pictures; **31,** (i) ©Phil Schermeister/ALLSTOCK; **32, 33,** ©David P. Maitland/Planet Earth Pictures; **34, 35,** ©Studiohio; **36,** ©KS Studios/1991; **37,** ©Brent Turner/BLT Productions/1991; **38,** (bl) L. West/Bruce Coleman, (br) Eric A. Soder/Tom Stack Associates; **39,** (t) Adam Jones/Natural Selection; (b) Milton Rand/Tom Stack Associates; **40, 41,** ©Jeff Topping/Space Biospheres Ventures; **42, 43,** ©Frans Lanting/ALLSTOCK; **43,** (i) ©David Scharf/Peter Arnold, Inc.; **44, 45,** ©Studiohio; **46,** (i) ©Peter Scoones/Planet Earth Pictures; **46, 47,** ©Jonathan Scott/Planet Earth Pictures; **47,** (tl) (tr) (mr) ©Ken Lucas/Planet Earth Pictures, (bl) ©David Kiger/Planet Earth Pictures, (bm) ©William M. Smithey, Jr./Planet Earth Pictures, (br) ©Bruce Coleman, Inc.; **48,** (tr) ©Art Wolfe/ALLSTOCK, (ml) Bruce Coleman, Inc./Cardoni, (b) ©Barry L. Runk/Grant Heilman Photography, Inc.; **49,** (tl) Bruce Coleman, Inc./Mardene Weisser, (r) ©Michael Ederegger/Peter Arnold, Inc., (b) ©Georgette Douwma/Planet Earth Pictures; **50,** (ml) Animals Animals/Zig Leszczynski, (br) ©Brent Turner/BLT Productions/1991; **50, 51,** ©Jonathan Scott/Planet Earth Pictures; **51,** (inset) Animals Animals/Breck P. Kent; **52,** (tl) ©Brian Parker/Tom Stack & Associates, (tm) ©John Gerlack/Tom Stack & Associates, (tr) Bruce Coleman, Inc./Bill Wood, (b) Bruce Coleman, Inc./Des & Jen Bartlett; **52, 53,** ©Tom Van Sant/The Geosphere Project, Santa Monica, CA; **53,** (l) ©Kevin Schafer/Martha Hill/Tom Stack & Associates, (r) Bruce Coleman, Inc./Hans Reinhard; **54, 55,** ©Gerry Ellis/The Wildlife Collection; **56, 57,** ©KS Studios; **57,** (b) ©Manfred Kage/Peter Arnold, Inc.; **58,** (t) Animals Animals/Johnny Johnson, (b) Wendy Shattil/Bob Rozinski ©1991; **59,** (t) Bruce Coleman, Inc./Joe McDonald, (b) ©Don & Esther Phillips/Tom Stack & Associates; **60,** (it) ©John Downer/Planet Earth Pictures, (ib) ©John Gerlach/Tom Stack & Associates; **60, 61,** ©Jeff March/Natural Selection; **62,** (it) ©Kim Heacox/Peter Arnold, Inc.; **62, 63,** ©C. Brown/Sipa Press; **63,** (it) ©Kennan Ward/Natural Selection; **64,** (inset) ©Pete Atkinson/Planet Earth Pictures; **66, 67,** ©Studiohio; **68,** (tr) ©Jerry Whaley/Natural Selection, (bl) Animals Animals/Stephen Dalton; **69,** ©David Dennis/Tom Stack & Associates, except (tr) Animals Animals/Breck P. Kent; **70,** (b) Bruce Coleman, Inc./John Visser; **70, 71,** (t) Animals Animals/Oxford Scientific films; **71,** (ml) ©Fred Bavendam/ALLSTOCK, (b) ©John Cancalosi/Natural Selection; **72,** (t) ©John Shaw/Tom Stack & Associates, (b) Animals Animals/Joe McDonald; **73,** (tl) Animals Animals/Zig Leszczynski; (mr) Bruce Coleman, Inc./Wolfgang Bayer, (b) ©Studiohio; **74,** (i) ©Art Wolfe/ALLSTOCK; **74, 75,** Bruce Coleman, Inc./Mark Sherman; **76, 77,** ©David Muench/ALLSTOCK; **78, 79,** ©Studiohio; **81,** (tr) ©KS Studios/1991; **82,** (i) ©Frans Lanting/ALLSTOCK; **82, 83,** ©KS Studios/1991; **84,** Animals Animals/Patti Murray, except (tr) Bruce Coleman, Inc.,/D. Overcash; **85,** Animals Animals/Zig Leszczynski, except (bm) Animals Animals/Breck P. Kent; **86,** (i) Bruce Coleman, Inc./M.P. Kahl; **86, 87,** ©C. Allan Morgan/Peter Arnold, Inc.; **88, 89,** ©Johnathan Scott/Planet Earth Pictures; **90, 91,** ©John Lythgoe/Planet Earth Pictures.

Illustration Credits:
14, 24(c), 34, 44, 56, 66, 78, Bob Giuliani; **24 (b),** James Shough; **18, 19,** Wendy Smith-Griswold; **27, 80, 81,** James Needham; **37,** Felipe Passalacqua; **38-39,** Barbara Wolff; **46, 65,** Lee M. Mejia; **88, 89,** Jan Wills